Tears in a Bottle

Tears in a Bottle

Stories of life and loss

Clair Hudson Jantzen

Order this book online at www.trafford.com
or email orders@trafford.com

Most Trafford titles are also available at major online book retailers.

Printed in the United States of America.

ISBN: 978-1-4269-3868-9 (sc)
ISBN: 978-1-4269-3869-6 (e)

Trafford rev. 09/06/2012

www.trafford.com

North America & international
toll-free: 1 888 232 4444 (USA & Canada)
phone: 250 383 6864 ♦ fax: 812 355 4082

To My Wife

Rachel

who has always been my
cheerleader and inspiration.

Psalm 56:8

You keep track of all my sorrows.
You have collected all my tears in your bottle.
You have recorded each one in your book.

FOREWORD

There is value to stories – to our narratives of grief. The experience of grief can be very isolating. In my years as a counselor, researcher, and writer about grief, I often have found that people have two possible theories of grief – implicit and explicit. The implicit theory is that each day after a loss, our grief ebbs a bit. We become a bit stronger; grief becomes a little more manageable. Others might have a more explicit theory of grief – perhaps building on a stage theory – thinking that grief is predictable, that we go through a series of stages in a predetermined amount of time, ultimately learning to accept our loss, forget what is past, and move on with our lives.

Yet, these models flounder when we truly experience loss. We find grief far more chaotic, far more individual, far more unpredictable than we imagined. We are beset by buzzing emotions. Our loss affects us on all levels – physically and spiritually, from the ways we think to how we behave.

That is the value of stories. This is the value of Clair Jantzen's *Tears in a Bottle*. For here we hear the real stories of people who are grieving. And these individual narratives have power.

First, they offer validation. As we hear the stories of others, it validates our own stories. It reminds us that our reactions are normal and natural responses to loss. As I lecture to community audiences on grief, the question I am asked most often is a variation of the question *Am I going crazy? It has been six months and my grief is worse. Am I going crazy?* These stories reaffirm that we are not going crazy – we are simply grieving.

Second, they offer suggestions for coping with loss. As we hear how others cope, we might find suggestions and counsel that can sustain us as we journey with grief.

Finally, these stories offer hope. They tell us at a time of deep difficulty that we are not alone – that we can and will live even after our loss.

Tears in a Bottle then ultimately becomes a tonic – something to carry with us, to use when our strength ebbs, as we journey with grief.

--Kenneth J. Doka, PhD

ACKNOWLEDGMENTS

The stories you are about to read are the real experiences of real people with whom I have travelled the road of suffering. Together we have learned what it means to have patience with the speed of the journey, to take in the shifting landscape that is bereavement and to find renewed hope for living. The names, genders, ages and circumstances have been changed to protect the suffering.

I would like to gratefully acknowledge the keen eye and skillful shutter hand of Susan Taylor of Kelowna, BC for the images in this book. Susan and I have walked the path of grief together as she and her husband, Dr. Tom Taylor, have laid to rest their mothers, both of whom suffered from Alzheimer's and subsequently died. Susan has kindly offered me access to her vast store of wonderful photography from around the world.

I'm also grateful to Mark Wiebe for his expertise in graphic design. I think his cover design is pretty cool. Thanks for your encouragement, Mark.

Most significant and deserving of my undying gratitude is my wife, Rachel, who has always been my greatest fan and cheer leader. Rachel, your faith in me has been a key factor in moving this work from hard drive space to print. Thank you, my love.

1   **THE CELEBRANT**

Before we begin the funeral service, I gather with the family in an anteroom to collect our thoughts and sometimes pray. To facilitate this I ask that we form a circle and grasp hands. Then I *break* the circle, to give the family a visual reminder that the family circle has been broken and that a hole has appeared against their will. It will take a long time to adjust to life without their loved one and for this they will need superhuman help.

"O God, getting used to living without _____ will take more energy than we can possibly conjure up. For this task we need you and we need you now. Please help us eventually to accept this loss, but for now, just help us to heal. Amen."

2

SALLY

They wonder why I'm not "over it" yet. What in the world do they mean? Do they mean, am I back to normal? Not crying my eyes out, wanting to die? No longer feeling pain? Not talking endlessly about my husband? I'll *never* get over this. If by getting over it they mean forgetting him, never tearing up at the mention of his name, or falling strangely quiet in a room full of chatting friends, no, I don't think so. No, normal for me would mean getting him back; that will not happen here on earth. So, no, I don't think I'll be getting over it.

3

SAM

Someone told a joke in the booth next to mine at Denny's while I picked at the bacon on my breakfast plate. I heard the punch line and laughed inside. Suddenly catching myself chortling away, I was immediately overcome with guilt. I shouldn't be enjoying myself yet. It's too soon. Boy, was that funny, though. When is it OK to laugh again? I don't know. It feels so strange to laugh, all I've been doing is crying. But it *did* feel good. Could I be healing? Could it be the agony has passed? Is there joy again? I wonder.

4 YVONNE

How are you doing? Keeping busy, I said. It's true, there's so much to do to tie things up. Tie things up. Close the book. Complete the chapter. Finish it off. Clean it up. No matter how you put it, it sounds so final. It is final. But why does it sound so awful? Because I didn't want it to be final. Oh, I knew the end would come, just didn't think I'd be the one to see it. Didn't want to be the first to go either, but here I am, finishing things up: bank accounts, clothes closets, land titles office, insurance, driver's license, and on and on. How am I doing? I'm busy, shutting it down, wrapping it up, and tying up loose ends.

5

FRED

What was that the minister said, something about the valley of death; or was it the valley of the *shadow* of death? Yes, that's it—walking through the valley of the shadow of death. I remember now. And he said the key word was 'through.' That's what he said, said we'd make it through. I'm not sure I will, but I haven't died yet like I thought I would; like I wanted to. No, not kill myself, just curl up and fade away, go away and be together again, with her. It's been a while now since that thought has preoccupied me; maybe I will make it through. Maybe, just maybe the Shepherd is helping me through this valley of the shadow of death.

6   CLAIR

It's always too soon to die. My nephew was born with no septum in his heart and died after struggling for 48 hours to live. My wife's grandfather lived to 107. We weren't done with her grandpa yet. We hadn't even started with Jordan. So when friends tried to console me at *my* grandfather's funeral, telling me to be grateful that he'd had a long life and that I'd had 89 years with him, I wasn't comforted. Because I wasn't finished with Grandpa yet. I think people said what they did to make *themselves* feel comfortable, not to comfort me. Be thankful he's not in pain anymore, they said. Oh yeah, well, if you want to talk to the dead guy, he's in the casket. *I'm* the one in pain. What comfort have you got for *me*?

7 DOROTHY

She was the perfect widow. All through the funeral, she was the perfect grieving widow—dabbing her eyes, smiling painfully. There's never an Oscar around when you deserve one. I knew better. As we drove around during the weeks after we buried him, she wanted to go places, anyplace. Old places, places they'd lived together, places they'd built. New places, places she hadn't seen in the years she'd driven from her place to his place, from their home to the care home. Day after day, year after year, same trip, same husband, less life. I said, "Aren't you just a bit relieved this 6 year ordeal is over?" Her 90 year old head whipped around and her sigh was palpable. No Oscar now. The gig was up. She didn't have to act anymore. The truth was out: It was OK to feel relieved that the grind of caring for him, of cooking for him, of sewing for him, of watching him deteriorate before her eyes, ever so slowly, was over. She was done watching the manhood seep ever so painfully from his body and his mind and his spirit. Watching him die. It was over. And she felt relieved. And someone else knew. And it was OK.

8   JUNE

I can't stand poems that tell us "don't stand at my grave and weep," or "when I'm gone, don't be sad, remember the good times." I think they're written by people who don't believe they made a difference to anybody. When I die, I sure hope someone cries. I want to know that I made a difference. Focusing on the positive and on the memories at the expense of recalling what I lost when Bobby died seems phony to me. I lost a whole lot the day they called me from his office that there'd been an accident and Bobby wasn't going to make it. I cried then, I cried at the funeral, I cried at the grave as his broken body was lowered into oblivion; I cried at the reception afterward, I cried in the limousine on the way home, I cried myself to sleep that night, and now, 10 months later I still stand at his grave and weep. The kids and I lost a whole lot the day Bobby left us.

9 JUNE

Let me tell you what I lost when Bobby died. I lost my lover. No more lovemaking at weird times of the day or night. No more holding each other's hands as we drive. No more butt-pinches in checkout lines at Safeway. No more racy cards with tender words penned in his characteristic block letters. Gone are the walks around the neighborhood after the kids are in bed. Gone are the dreams of finally getting to some exotic place and making love in broad daylight on a deserted sun-dappled beach. When Bobby died, my arms emptied of the man that made my world a livable place because of his passion for me. Hold on to the memories and smile? Sure, but first let me hold on to the memories and cry because they remind me of how terribly I have lost.

10 TIM

They tell me I'll eventually heal from this wound called death. I'm not so sure. I feel wounded, but I remember when I sliced my finger with that crazy box knife trying to open the parcel from the folks. We disinfected it, put ointment on it, bound it up tight and waited. Eventually my body's clotting inclinations overcame the bleeding and when the scab fell off 10 days later, you could almost see the daily advances of the healing process. No, Sharon's death is more like...like an

 amputation. The whole finger...no, the whole arm off, gone, gone forever, leaving me with phantom pains that are so real I could scream. And I scream, burying my face in the pillow lest I scare the heck out of the kids. No prosthesis would ever work like the real thing and no one else will be like Sharon. Sharon is gone. Woe is me.

11

JUNE

You know what else I lost when Bobby died? I lost my friend. No more teasing me about my turned down toes. No more wrestling with the check book. No more prayers whispered in the dark for the kids to turn out right. No more vacations to plan. Gone is my burger-flipper, my oil-changer, my picture-hanger, my Christmas tree finder. Gone is my kids' daddy, my Mr. Fixit, my driver, my buddy, my companion and my friend. No wonder I'm so torn apart. No wonder I can hardly catch my breath sometimes. No wonder I stare hollow-eyed out the window like I did last summer when he went to Phoenix for the weeklong convention, waiting for him to come home to me, knowing that he would come back, knowing now that he never will, wishing that he would.

12

SUE

Given the nature of her loss, this young mother was a bit too 'together.' Losing the healthier of twin girls, you'd think she'd be at least *somewhat* distraught. As we discussed the details of the memorial service for three-month old Jennie, a thought kept nagging at me.

"Who found Jennie that morning?" I asked.

"I did."

"What did you do?"

"I screamed and called for Jerry. He came and tried to revive her, but it was obvious...." She could not finish.

"Then what?"

"We called 911 and they took the baby away."

"Sue, when's the last time you held Jennie?"

"Haven't, I guess, since I rocked her to sleep last night."

"Would you like to now?"

"No, it would be too hard."

"Yes, I know, but would you like to? Would you like to hold her and say goodbye to her?"

"Yes, I would."

I retrieved the lifeless form of her baby from our morgue, wrapped in a blanket, tiny pink face, dark lips parted, and delicate long lashes damp with the cold of death. As I entered the room, the sobs came from deep within her, slow and trembling, then anguished and terrible. Having placed Jennie in Sue's waiting arms, I told her to take as long as she needed, then stepped softly out of the room. The heaving cries tore at my heart and squeezed the tears out mercilessly. For three or four minutes she wept; then she gradually quieted down. The child's grandmother opened the door and beckoned. Sue was gently cradling little Jennie on her shoulder as if she were burping her, stroking her back and head, rocking back and forth, eyes closed and mouthing the words, "There, there, it's all OK now. We're both OK now." Then without another word she passed the child to me and sat down.

13   SHEILAGH

I dread getting the mail. I used to love the walk to the end of the drive, about 100 yards of smoothly packed white stone, meticulously laid by my husband. Our driveway is lined with stout maples, now fire red in the shortened days of autumn, each small sapling lovingly placed by two people still very much in love after thirty-seven years, six years of high school naïveté and college bliss, and thirty-one lightening fast years of marriage. Now with each step toward the roadway, my heart grows heavier. Oh, I fully expect that there'll be a couple of cards from folks that weren't at the funeral service. What I dread is seeing the envelopes; well, not the envelopes but the address. Well, not the address, I love our address, 100 Centennial Drive. The first line of the address. Oh, I like my name well enough. Sheilagh's a good strong name for a strong woman, my father used to say. No, it's just so hard for me to see the word in front of my name on all those envelopes: *Mrs.* Mrs. Sheilagh Branson. Some of the envelopes even say Mrs. Frank Branson. I dread seeing my name in all of its forms. Mrs. Branson meant I was *married.* Mrs. Frank Branson meant I was married to *Mr.* Frank Branson. Mrs. Sheilagh Branson meant I was not Sheilagh *Burrows,* but Sheilagh *Branson.* Sheilagh Branson meant I was Sheilagh, but Sheilagh used to include Frank because we were one—not a twosome, but a 'one-some.' Now Frank is gone and I'm having a hard time finding Sheilagh. I get the mail, but halfway back from the box I usually collapse and sit down under a maple to cry tears of confusion. Hot drops of agony fall on the letters, smudging all the Mr.'s and Mrs.', the Sheilagh's, the Frank's and the Branson's. "Oh, Frank, who in the world am I without you?"

14 SHARLENE

The ringing phone pulled me from my reverie. Bill Penner said something about dropping by this afternoon. I said that would be fine, and hung up. When the door bell sounded at two o'clock, it seemed amazing that 3 hours could have passed since he called. Couldn't remember a thing I'd done in that time. Seems I'm forgetting more and remembering less since my Howie died. I ushered Bill to the sofa and went looking for my glasses. After 5 or 6 minutes of hunting, I found them...on the table, next to the sofa!

An envelope lay on the arm of the chair I'd sat in. Snoopy was smiling at me. Get Met. It Pays.

I lost it. Just four years ago, Howie and I had met Bill quite by accident in Puerto Vayarta. Both from the same city, we spent the next week and a half with him and Marsha and became fast friends. The day I got pregnant with Shawn, Bill talked life insurance with Howie and in no time a $350 thousand policy was in place. Now, too, it was in place...in front of me, and all I could do was cry. I remember feeling angry with Bill for bringing it up to the house. I let him have it, both barrels. He just sat there and listened to me, his eyes misting over. When I was done, he leaned over, took my freckled hand in his and said, "I miss him too." Bless you, Bill. You didn't deserve my anger, but you understood that it wasn't directed at you but at the accident that took Howie from me. You accepted my anger—accepting me and my pain. And because you accepted me, I could see your pain too. You loved Howie as well. Thanks for the hug. And thanks for bringing the cheque. Thanks for loving us and being there for us in this tangible way.

15   JARED

"I got rid of everything right away," he said. "Boxed it up and out it went. It was better that way." I glanced over to see who was speaking and was surprised to see how young he was. Nice suit, shoes. Armani, Gucci. I wondered whom he'd lost. He was talking so loudly to his companion; I felt that over-hearing was hardly eavesdropping. My own Cheryl was gone for three and a half months and I still couldn't entertain the thought of removing anything from our room. Her scent was everywhere. I'd taken to sleeping on her side of the bed. It was such a comfort. Her robe still hung in our ensuite on its hook. I'd steal a whiff of her before leaving for work each day. Get rid of her things? Was I enshrining her? Was I weird?

"Took me about 8 months before I got up the jam to part with April's things," replied the companion. "Just having them there around me really helped me heal up. Bob and June and I went through everything last weekend. It was the right time."

OK, so I'm not weird. I'm just not in a hurry.

16 JORDAN

The two boys stood staring into the casket. The older had a knowing look on his face; the younger, about 7, his head cocked to one side, appeared somewhat quizzical. "Is Grandma sleeping?" he asked.

"No, she's dead."

"Oh." Silence. "What do you mean? She looks like she's sleeping, 'cept she's got her glasses on. She never slept with glasses."

"'Course not," retorted the older boy, whom I guessed to be about 10. "But she's dead, so she can do what she wants. And she wants her glasses on."

"Oh." Silence. "When will she wake up? Is she coming to the supper afterward?"

"Jordan, she's dead. Dead people don't eat and she's not coming to the supper! Look, you remember the Lion King?"

"Yeah, I like that one."

"Remember when Simba's daddy was lying down in the brambles after the stampede of wildebeests and couldn't get up? He was dead."

"Oh, I get it." And with that, little Jordan turned to me, as I was the closest adult to him, and said emphatically: "Grandma got run over by a herd of wildebeests!"

17   BREANNA

The counselor could hardly believe what he was hearing. Breanna's mother, dying of a heart attack; then twenty-two days later, her husband, Frank, dying in his sleep—an aneurism.

"I didn't know what else to do. He didn't want the kids at his Mom's funeral because it would be too hard for them to see her in the casket. So when Frank died," she sobbed, "I just did the same thing and sent them to my friend's again. Now they're so full of questions about who took Daddy and Grandma away. And why would I let Daddy go to heaven in his underwear? They had been awakened with the commotion of the paramedics trying to revive him and then taking him out of the house. He slept in his favorite boxers—the ones I got him on our honeymoon in Florida—fluorescent, with 'Voulez-vous?' all over them. They think he's in heaven in his boxers! Can you believe it? Do you think it would have been better to have let them see him at the funeral home in the casket? I mean, I did. He looked so good in his pinstriped suit. Like a Roman god, my Frank, black hair..." She couldn't continue. When she'd calmed down a bit, she carried on. "I should have let them come, don't you think? I think so. Then at least they wouldn't be imagining things. They're so imaginative, aren't they?"

18   **CLAIR**

When my son was two and a half years old, he had 4 plastic drills, but wanted to play with the real thing. So I decided that if he was going to play with it, I'd teach him to use it. He could plug it in. He could select a bit, insert it correctly, and tighten it (relatively). He could place a screw on the end, stand up and then drive it into a two-by-four.

One day, while playing with the drill, he dropped it on his big toe. Major owie. The toe turned black. Not a day went by without a comment on the big owie. If someone came to visit, he'd come see who it was, size things up and begin the announcement: "Big owie....Big owie....BIG owie....BIG OWIE." If you didn't notice him, the volume went up. "BIG OWIE!!" Should you fail to acknowledge, you'd likely get a poke in the leg. The moment his owie was attended to by someone new, he was gone. Satisfied.

Unless he has the significance of this event in his life established, he is emotionally incapable of moving on. That is what Grandpa's funeral did for us. It permitted us to mark the event in time and space as something of significance. It gave friends a chance to come alongside us and say, in effect, "There, there. We notice. We care."

19

ANDY

"Well, you're right," Andy said. "The anticipation *was* worse than the actual day. I was expecting this really black time, but when I went up to the cemetery and laid a rose on her grave, it was alright, you know. Not as bad as I thought. I'm glad I had something planned, like you said. It helped to have something specific to do about my feelings on the anniversary of her death. I'm glad I didn't just let the day slip by without taking charge of it. It really is true that grief doesn't happen in stages. Taking responsibility for my journey and choosing to remember her, to embrace the pain, not to isolate myself by grieving alone, has been a life saver for me."

20   JANIE

We sat across from each other at the White Spot, poking at the eggs that looked back at us, wide-eyed from the plate. Janie's right hand gripped her fork; her left hand twirled her diamond engagement ring round and round next to her wedding band. "It's the silliest thing," she was saying, pulling me out of my reverie.

"What is?" I responded.

"Wearing a wedding band when you're not married. I mean, Darrell died over a year ago, but I still feel like I'm married. But you know, I was imagining not having them on the other day, and suddenly I felt so shameful, as if not wearing them was a betrayal of Darrell. As if I were saying, 'I never knew you.' I felt terrible about it, so I kept them on. Is that strange, or what?"

"I don't know," I replied. "Jacquie still wears hers and it's been over 4 years since Buck was killed. Doesn't seem strange to see them on her."

"Yeah, you're right," said Janie. "But Judy wears Tom's ring along with hers around her neck on that chain he brought back for her from Australia. Nothing wrong with that."

"No, there isn't. Maybe it's an individual thing. What's good for one isn't good for someone else." I poked at the eggs again. I wasn't hungry anymore.

21 THE HEALTH MANUAL

The Health Manual was produced by our provincial government and delivered to our door. Rifling through it, I was impressed with the multitude of subjects it covered and the helpful information I would have at my fingertips. "I wonder what they say about grieving," I thought. The index scared me—one page. "Well, quality is more important than quantity," I said to myself as I flipped to the appropriate section. Not one page, not one column, but one paragraph. "The content better be substantial!" Physical symptoms of grief and one pathetic last sentence: "If these symptoms persist for more than four weeks following your loss, consult your physician." Thanks!

22 THREE FRIENDS

The three men around the table were sharing with me their stories. It became clear very quickly that though each had lost his wife, and that each woman had succumbed to cancer, their journeys were unique. They told of how their wives had suffered and died, in one case, over a period of seven years. A common thread, however, in each tale of woe was the fact that none of the three had ever shared her true feelings and fears with her man. And to a man they told me that they had felt 'protected'. The hard part, they said, for their wives, was not the dying itself, but watching their husbands watch them die. In an effort to shield them from increased pain, they bore it themselves and spared their husbands the truth of their innermost pain.

23   **GEOFFREY**

"I can't imagine ever feeling any different than I do now. I keep looking for the light at the end of the tunnel, but all I can see is a black hole. Will it ever end? My friends think I'm doing better, getting 'on top of it,' but they only see me at my best. It's been seven months since she died, and it still seems as black as the day she was diagnosed—a two year long black tunnel with no end in sight. I keep seeing the sores, I can smell them. It was awful; I can't get the smell out of my mind. I didn't know the mind could retain smells."

24   **THE KIDS**

Scotty was just two months old when he died of SIDS, Valerie, only 35, of cancer, leaving a husband and 2 kids. Jordan fell from the bridge on July the 4th. He was 16 and he never did see the fireworks. Chrissy was just 13, severely handicapped, when she got stuck in her hospital bed and choked before morning came. It's not supposed to be this way. Children aren't supposed to die. You shouldn't have to bury your children. Death should have wrinkles.

25 BRYAN

Crying is good, they say. It's OK to cry. Sorrow equals tears. Don't keep it all bottled up, I've been told. It'll leak out somewhere else. If I keep my tears to myself, and don't let them out, I'll get ulcers. If I don't cry, people will think I'm not really missing her. It's good to cry, they say, because it means I'm healing.

Well, if crying is so good for me, I must be the healthiest guy in town. I've sure cried a lot.

26   **CLIFF**

Cliff told me how wonderful everyone was. The doctors were so sensitive, knowledgeable and helpful. The nurses were so thoughtful and caring. Friends loved on him and his dying wife, Abby; they hugged and even prayed for them. One young girl brought a fresh garden rose each morning to help them greet the day.

The day she died...it all stopped. Not a soul has called, sent a card or flower, prayed or hugged Cliff or even noticed him since Abby's bed was emptied and another took her place to die.

27   **GLORIA**

If only I would have done more. If only I could have known. He was doing so well after his surgery. If only I hadn't brought him home, though. I should have known he wasn't going to make it at home. He should have never left the hospital. I should have known he was going to have that clot. I should have sensed it. Now it's too late. I should have known, I should have seen.

Do you mean that you should have been more than you are? More than a woman? More than a nurse? More than a doctor? More than God?

28 AMBER

Seven year old Amber came to our children's grief group because she couldn't sleep at night. Ever since her brother was killed, her personality changed. Her appetite had vanished and she was losing weight. She never smiled. She had lost her sparkle. The upside was that she became a very obedient child, though her responses were dutiful.

As we colored our way through several sessions, attempting to identify her feelings, it became clear that Amber was "totally responsible" for Andrew's death. He was hit by a speeding driver hurtling down Glenview Road. Hit at 50 miles per hour on a cross walk as he and his friends tried to duck into the park.

Earlier he had been grounded. Amber had no recollection of the reason. Just that he was supposed to stay in. Dad and Mom were in the den watching Jeopardy when Andrew paused in her doorway, index finger laid on his lips, swearing her to secrecy. Wide-eyed she nodded. As she nods to me now the tears come. "I should have told them. It's all my fault."

29 MARTA

Sometimes I wonder why the heavens load up someone's plate more fully than others. In the space of 2 years Marta lost her father to congestive heart failure, her brother was murdered, then her mother took her own life. Barely had she begun to come out of her intense sorrow over Dad's death when she was stunned by her brother's sudden and violent death. She was still reeling from that loss when her mother chose her own time, adding still more weight to the unbearable pressure on Marta. She was now numb, thankfully in shock as her psyche shut down parts of her fragile being to take inventory and prevent mental and spiritual overload. She was encouraged to hear that what some 'friends' called being calloused, was really just shock and numbness, which would eventually give way to the bleeding of grief, which, having run its course would then turn to profound sadness.

30   **JOEY AND CINDI**

Joey and Cindi sat still as in turn, each member of the new group introduced himself and shared the reason for his being there. Some were quite taciturn; others barely uttered a word and were engulfed with emotion. But each one shared his or her story and then listened to a neighbor share. Joey told of the loss of his best friend in a car crash on the way home from a rock climbing trip. Geoff was instantly killed as the semi crossed the road into their path. Joey sustained head injuries. "I don't know why I'm here to tell you this, because I don't remember a thing about the accident. They tell me I'm different, and gradually I'm beginning to remember some of who I was. I miss Geoff, and I miss me."

Then Cindi spoke. "I'm here because I lost the man I married." There is a living, ongoing kind of death, every bit as real and painful as death itself.

31   **WENDY**

She didn't stay long in our group. She felt sort of out of place. Hearing the others share what losses had brought them to the group, she became more and more uncomfortable. She didn't come back.

I remembered some of the circumstances of her husband's ignoble death, drowning in his own vomit, face on the floor beside the toilet, his liver pickled from years of alcohol abuse. Wendy never cried that I could remember. She never really looked you in the eye, either. It seemed to me she was trying to come to terms with ambivalent feelings. I realized that her discomfort with the group had to do with her sense of shame that she felt so relieved that her ordeal was over. She felt bad that she didn't miss him. Nick had long ago lost her heart when he gave his to Ms. Tequila. She reluctantly took a holiday, tentatively giving way to the enjoyment of new places and sights. Gingerly she passed through the turbulence of freedom and shame, of liberation and loss, of missing 'what should have been' and anticipating 'what was yet to come.' She found her way to happiness again and I was reminded that grief looks different every time.

32   **LAWRENCE**

"I can't stay there and I can't sell it," said Lawrence of the spacious condo he and Edith had occupied for the ten years of their retirement. "If I stay in the house, I'm surrounded by memories, and I cry all day long. I can't imagine selling the place and having no memories at all. That's where she sat and read while I watched the basketball game. That's where she made the pies that our whole family is missing. And on the deck is where she grew the flowers that are dying because I haven't a clue what to do with them. So I go to my daughter's house and eat with her. I can't stand to see her toothbrush, nor can I bear to throw it out and see only mine. I feel like Kuwait," he jokes, "caught between Iraq and a hard place."

33   JOHNNY

Johnny cries as soon as I walk through the door. He is a man whose emotions are just beneath the surface. In fact, I think he's cried almost every time we've been together over the last 3 years. Johnny doesn't cry, though, because of the memories of what he's lost. Johnny cries because his wife's death means he can't continue to make things right. You see, Johnny wasn't a very good husband, most of the time. In fact, he was abusive. But she stuck with him, rightly or wrongly, and gave him yet another chance, which he took. But, oh so suddenly, she suffered a massive heart attack and died as they worked together in their business. "I didn't deserve her, and she didn't deserve what I did to her." The shame is palpable. So Johnny cries. And so he should, because that is what Johnny's grief is all about.

34   **SHEILA**

Sheila was dry-eyed most of the time I knew her. Doug's death was almost anticlimactic for her, though it was devastating for the boys. He'd been ill for so long and increasingly dependent, despondent and distant. With each passing day, a seething belligerence set in, toxic criticism of her, of the boys, of their level of care, and of his worsening condition. Then it became dangerous and she had to make the difficult choice to leave for awhile. The end came quickly. By the time he passed away, she was mostly relieved that the meanness was over. She rued the day of his diagnosis, for it was then, not when he died, that she'd lost her husband. He died to her long before he died to the world.

35   VICTOR AND LILLIE

They sat there, for all the world like two grandparents, fully expecting several rambunctious kids to come running in and plop themselves on waiting laps to ask for money for ice-cream. Though they looked like grandparents, they were childless, having witnessed the slow and painful decline of their son into the seamy underworld of big city drug life. Eventually the moment they had dreaded came: "This is Constable Holmes. I regret to inform you..." Then, within a year, they received a second visit informing them of a freeway accident which claimed the life of their only remaining child, their daughter. Not only would the grandchildren not come running, the children wouldn't come home either. Childlessness—giving them life and giving them up. Raising them and losing them. Sending them into the world to live on their own, to die prematurely.

36   ASHLEE

"Hi, my name is Ashlee and I'm here because I lost my husband to cancer one month ago today. I not only lost my husband, I lost my friend, my ride to work, my colleague at the University, my ride home, my everything, literally. There's no place I can go, no routine to continue which doesn't smell, look, feel like him, or inundate me with him. I can't be at home, go to work, be at work, come home from work, nor be at home again without constantly being in touch with what I have lost. This is actually the first place I've been in a month where I've never been with him. And because I'm talking about him—because this is a 'me', not a 'we' place—I feel hopeful that I may find more of these. As much as I long to be 'us' again, ironically, I need 'me' places so I can heal."

37 HEATHER

Anger seethed just under the surface as Heather told her story. "They wouldn't let me near, wouldn't let me touch him." Her husband had been crushed in a giant mixer on the jobsite. Workers, paramedics and police kept her back once she'd arrived on the scene after having been called by his boss. They physically restrained her from approaching the awful cauldron of death which had almost completely swallowed his body. "I just wanted to see him again, to touch him; I didn't care what he looked like. They kept saying it was for my own good. "You don't want to see him like that," they said. How could they possibly know what I wanted and didn't want? I wanted to see him and touch him and they wouldn't let me. I am so mad I could spit."

38   DAWN

Dawn's marriage hadn't been great but she'd had ten years with him. He hadn't been as warm and affectionate as when she'd first met him; she'd been quite disillusioned. But she'd made a promise she intended to keep. Then cancer stole the last two years. Looking after him as he died took time and effort away from her job and she had to take a leave of absence. His life waned before her eyes and soon he died. The lawyer called for the reading of the will. As she entered the spacious office, she sucked in her breath quickly and her heart pounded, for there in the room were his ex-wife and her 4 adult children. "What are they doing here?" she thought, but held her tongue. At 54, she couldn't afford any surprises financially, but she was totally unprepared for what came down that day. He'd left not a thing to her, not even the house. The sorrow over his death and her ensuing aloneness turned to gall and bitterness. She wanted to kill him but he was already dead. Dawn's grief journey had taken a precipitous detour. Though she'd never felt truly loved by him, she'd been faithful and kind, 'til death do us part.' He'd been well off and as the end drew near, she knew she wouldn't be destitute on her own. But the hammer had fallen and she was back at work, struggling between reluctant forgiveness and seething bitterness.

39 LESLIE

Within the space of five weeks over Easter and into early spring, Leslie went from being a vivacious fifteen year old beauty, to catching a cold, to having the flu, getting pneumonia, going into a coma and dying of a mystery illness. But instead of bitterness and emptiness, there appeared in Tim and Monica a poignant sadness along with a peaceful hope, a confident realization that God hadn't now become their enemy, but still wanted to be their friend, as he had been all along. *He* hadn't changed, just their family and their circumstances had.

40 BRENDA LEE

What carried me through the long months of his cancer was his amazing sense of humor. He could see the funny side of everything and that helped lighten the load of the awful things that were happening to his body as he wasted away. When they amputated his leg, he'd joke and tell his buddies to keep an eye out for a lone shoe on the highway. "I could use some of those."

41

PHOEBE

The worst thing about her twenty-five year old husband's death, according to Phoebe, was not that he took his own life. It was what his death meant: that he wouldn't be around for the birth of their fourth child and for the enjoyment of his children. She felt sorry for his misjudgment of the situation that sent him into a tailspin of self-condemnation. As it turned out, things weren't as bad as they seemed, and had he endured even a day or so, he would have seen it, too. I watched with glistening eyes as she proudly cut the ribbon on opening day of the business that together they had started—and which she brought to fruition.

42   **AL**

It wasn't her death that brought the tears to his eyes as we sat in the small living room of the condo that was their last home together. It wasn't even that he'd had to move her to a private hospital for care. His most profound sadness surrounded his memories of the day she told him he couldn't sleep with her in the same bed. He thought it odd, but decided not to push it and slept on the sofa in the living room where we now sat. Next night, the same. Then it dawned on him that she must think that he was their eldest son. Of course he couldn't sleep there. It would be inappropriate. The following night she came to him, tweaked his toes while he slept, and said, "What are you doing out here? Fall asleep watching TV or something?" Then Al cried. His lover had lost track of her lover.

43   **BRITTANY**

"I don't know what to do," said Brittany. "I'm having issues with my daughter, Brette. Since Tom's death, it seems I've become her worst enemy. She is so angry. I want to grieve; but she doesn't. She doesn't want to go to school. She went from being a straight 'A' student and on the principal's list, to failing her subjects, just because she's not showing up." The group's response was insightful. Brittany gained some insight into the remarkably different ways in which Brette was grieving: predominantly by lashing out in anger. And Brette was finding a safe place in Mom to vent her anger at the injustice of having to give up her Daddy. "This isn't about me, then," she responded. "I've been grieving myself and feeling her anger as additional injustice toward me, her wanting to hurt and punish me. I see now, that this is more about being a safe haven for her, a punching bag for her to unload her grief. I can do that. So should I just hold her and tell her I love her?" "Yes, and embrace her pain while you momentarily set aside yours. She's just a child, trying to be mature, but not succeeding. In some ways, in her fear, she has reverted to her childhood and is having a major temper tantrum which may last awhile. As long as you are still her rock, she'll be OK. The trouble is: you have no husband to go to for relief. That's why *we're* here. We'll help carry you."

44 NELLIE

Nellie's eyes moistened as she told me that she still couldn't go near the coffee pot. She'd had two cups of coffee in the month since he'd died, one at Joan's next door and one cup of instant that she instantly threw out, it tasted so terrible. "He used to get up first and make me a cup of coffee and we'd gossip for a while in bed before getting up. That's why I still can't stand to go near the coffee pot. You see, if I make my own coffee, then he's really gone."

45   **MARION**

"I can still smell her," said Marion. "One of the last things the nurses asked was if there was something of Mom's I wanted to take with me, and I said I'd take her rings. Do you know that I wear them all the time on a chain around my neck? I shower with them. It's been 5 months since she died and they still have her smell on them. It's incredibly comforting."

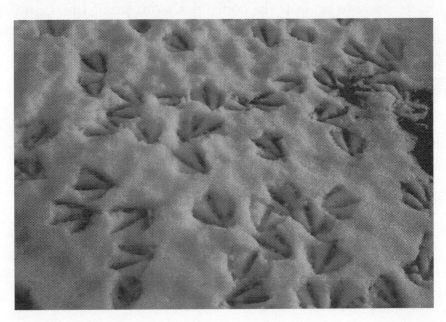

46　　ELFRIEDE

When Hans died, I wanted to curl up in a ball and die. I wasn't suicidal; I just didn't want to live with this pain. Within a week I developed chest pains, really bad. Sometimes it hurt so much I could hardly breathe. I called my doctor, who ran some tests, but nothing. A few days later, more pain. But this time I waited. They worsened and I called my friend to take me to the hospital. It was on the way there that I realized I wanted to live. It was the awareness that subconsciously I was taking care of *me*, and that my mind and body were helping to keep me alive. Yes, I decided, I will keep living.

47 SYBIL

"I find it so interesting," said Grandma recently as we drove up the mountain to see the Christmas lights. "Jacob and I used to visit with so many couples. We had so many friends. And none of them have invited me over since he died. I get together with the girls (3 other widows) all the time, but with the married couples, never. I wonder why that is? I see them in church, but they don't see me. And we never get together. It's so sad."

48   **MARTY**

"Short term energy relieving behaviors," said the facilitator, "are those things we do to anesthetize ourselves repeatedly from the pain; things like keeping busy, shopping, consuming alcohol, food or prescription drugs."

"And those things are wrong?" asked Marty.

"Well, it's not that. It's just that they don't work in the long run. One has to plow *through* the pain."

"Hmm. I take 2 sleeping pills and a glass of wine before going to bed. There's no way I'm waking up at night."

Apparently, the mere mention of the long term effects of anesthetizing one's pain robbed her pattern of its power. She returned next week and announced that she was down to one sleeping pill. The group cheered her bravery.

"But I'm up to two glasses of wine!" Much healthy laughter ensued. "Just kidding," she said.

49

SAM

"When I die, don't make a fuss over me, just cremate me and scatter the ashes. I don't want a funeral service at all," said Sam.

The next summer, his beautiful, free-spirited young daughter, Tiffany died inexplicably in her sleep; and Sam was broken. "I need to have a service," said Martha, his distraught wife. "I've got to do something to heal my heart." "Well, you go ahead, but don't count on me for input. I can't do it."

So Martha did. The minister, a volunteer firefighter, drove up in a fire truck, as his personal vehicle was in the shop. After helping to plan the memorial, he stopped in the driveway to chat briefly. "Think of what you want to say at the memorial, Sam. Put some thought into it, write it out." "Are you nuts? I could never do that." "Well, I'd encourage you strongly to think about it and at least put your thoughts on paper, so that I can read them for you if you can't."

The music, the butterflies, the tributes, the atmosphere, the friends, the embraces, and even Sam's hesitantly delivered eulogy to his baby girl went better than he'd expected. "You know, I've changed my mind about the service. Being there with all those people took away that big pain in my heart." Talking later at night, they realized that they'd both always regretted not memorializing Sam's dad when he died in 1976.

50 GEORGE

"She was only 44. Her death was awful, and perhaps, even preventable. It certainly wasn't diagnosed as early as it could have been. But I don't know. Do I feel cheated? No. If you're an active player in the game, I guess you might feel cheated. But when you realize you really have no control, it's different. I felt sorry for Sylvia. She was so like the kid who doesn't want to go to bed early. There might be pizza and she'd miss a slice.

It was so hard to watch her die. She went from age 40 to age 80 in the space of about 3 months. The toughest thing was seeing a person so disassembled. Piece by piece she came apart, like going to the scrap yard with your car, week after week. First you return without the fenders; then the bumpers are gone and next time the windshield. It was really hard."

51   RUTH

Grief is about forgetting, about envy, about being alone in a crowd. Grief has a mind of its own, rendering the griever out of control of his choices, his thoughts, and his emotions.

"I can't multitask anymore," said Ruth, who was used to cooking, grandparenting and running a business at the same time. "I get lost and can't remember what I was doing from one minute to the next. I envy those women whose husbands are still there for support, companionship and help. I feel terribly alone when I'm with my family or in any group of people."

Then I reminded her that she *was* multitasking, just in a different way. On top of all the things she was still valiantly attempting to accomplish, she had added the task of grieving too, not to mention half the things her husband used to do.

ABOUT THE AUTHOR

Clair Jantzen has a Master of Arts in Counseling and has been in practice for over 30 years. He lives with his wife, Rachel, of 25 years, and their son in Kelowna, British Columbia, Canada. They also have one married daughter. Clair is currently a grief counselor and chaplain in a funeral home where he also facilitates grief support care. He is a Registered Counselor, a member of the Canadian Professional Counselors Association and is the author of *Living with Grief, Children and Adolescents: The Value of the Funeral Service and Viewing.* For more information see www.clairjantzen.ca

Over the course of his career, Clair has had the opportunity to care for thousands of bereaved individuals who have shared their stories of loss and the challenges of adjusting to life without their loved ones. One of the struggles that the newly bereaved encounter is an inability to concentrate. Many times they purchase or are given a book on grief which they find difficult to get through because they are too preoccupied to focus. This book provides a simple way for them to digest the accounts of others on the journey of loss in the form of one page vignettes and stimulating photography. It can sit by the bedside or on the coffee table and be consumed in bite-size portions which can be mused upon for a minute, an hour or a day, before continuing.